Welcoming the Stranger

Signposts for Building Bridges and Making Peace

Nick Regnault

Contact South West Baptist Church

Web: **https://www.swbc.org.nz/**

Email: **info@swbc.org.nz**

Post: PO Box 33048, Barrington, Christchurch 8244

Print-on-demand edition 2019

ISBN 978-1-71-193587-4

Philip Garside Publishing Ltd
PO Box 17160
Wellington 6147
New Zealand

bookspgpl@gmail.com   www.pgpl.co.nz

eBook editions also available

Front cover photograph
Alexander Garside—Garside Imaging

Contents

Endorsement from Tearfund

My immediate response to the terror attacks in Christchurch was to turn to the Church.

Tearfund emerged from the Church and exists for the Church, to bring relief to those who need it the most, no strings attached. When crisis strikes, anywhere in the world, we first look to God's people living in those places, and ask "how can we best help you to serve the most vulnerable in your communities?"

In the hours following the Mosque attacks, that's the question I asked Alan Jamieson, Senior Pastor at South West Baptist, as I wondered how God's people in Christchurch would choose to respond to this extreme act of violence.

I believe God's people have made beautiful choices in how they have responded to this horrible act of terror. I believe the choices South West Baptist have made – and which they continue to make – will have meaningful and enduring impact in Aotearoa New Zealand. I am grateful they have gone to the effort to tell their story.

In this book Nick humbly reflects on the experience of befriending people of different cultures and beliefs, and what it has meant for South West Baptist to journey with them through their pain and grief. I encourage you to read this short book and to reflect on what God is saying about reaching out and building bonds of friendship with the people He has placed around you.

Ian McInnes, CEO Tearfund

Acknowledgements

I would like to thank my community of South West Baptist Church without whom the experiences reflected upon in this book would not exist. I am also very thankful for the support and encouragement of my colleagues in the Resettlement Team, particularly Alan Jamieson, Elizabeth Peters, Katie Kingsthwaite, Murdoch Stephens and Nancy Yuan, who contributed to the research, made useful suggestions and generally made this book a whole lot better.

Thank you to Modar and Ramia: invaluable sources of information on the experience of resettling from the Middle East to New Zealand; always patient with our questions.

Thanks to the generosity of the Lang Centre for Civic and Social Responsibility (**https://www.swarthmore.edu/lang-center/**), all profits from the sale of this book will be used to support the community sponsorship of refugees in Aotearoa New Zealand.

Foreword by Te Raranga

We all like to feel included, connected, and valued as part of a wider family, neighbourhood or community. Recognising that starting over in a new place and making that 'place' feel truly 'ours,' can be a daunting and sometimes a slow process. For those of us who lived through the Christchurch earthquakes, we quickly realised in new ways how important it was to have connections with those around us, and how much easier it became coping with uncertainty and stress when you felt you were in it together with others. Te Raranga – the churches networking to bless our city – was born out of recognition that connecting people and communicating well went a long way to building stronger and healthier communities. Whether as individuals, families, churches, businesses or organisations, each of us is a strand that can be woven together to form something greater than ourselves.

Te Raranga is delighted to be supporting the Refugee Resettlement initiatives that are grounded in community, and that seek to build bridges between people of different cultures, race, and faith. The reflections from South West Baptist Church, and their journey in welcoming refugee families to Christchurch, highlight the powerful contribution anyone can make, by offering friendship in intentional ways, recognising and honouring diversity and independence, and valuing mutual learning and growth. By extending friendship and inclusion, we find ourselves enriched and our communities strengthened and empowered.

As faith communities we reach out to others in recognition that our loving God reached out to us – extended community, welcome, and inclusion. Compassion extends a welcome, not for recognition or reward, not with set expectations or strings attached, but because that is the very nature of compassion; the very nature of God lived out in his people.

There is wise counsel here. Temper the urge to jump into the detail and practicalities, before committing to some hard conversations around motives and values, honesty around personal bias and cultural stereotypes. The signposts offered in this book provide a valuable springboard for those seeking to support migrants and refugees, and wanting to build resilient, caring communities. This needs to be a journey for the long haul, not a knee jerk reaction or short-term emotional response. But in choosing to commit to journey together with others we will gain so much more than we ever give.

Ken Shelley

Te Raranga

Introduction

Ordinary people going about their daily lives can make an extraordinary difference in the lives of others – and simultaneously enrich their own lives. These are my reflections from observing and hearing stories from people living in intentional and active ways to reach out to others of different cultural background living amongst us. People that see that there are opportunities in their lives to include others and in doing so, become part of a rich web of connections that create meaning, comfort and belonging for us all.

Like much of New Zealand, the terror attacks on the Al Noor and Linwood mosques in Christchurch on 15 March 2019 caused us to reflect on who we are and on the society of which we are part. People seemed to want stronger community feeling, less isolation and racism, and a New Zealand that was a safe and welcoming place. It sounded like people wanted places of inclusion, where everyone had space and opportunity to experience, give and receive love and acceptance.

In the weeks following the tragic events, we were encouraged by the outpouring of gifts, actions, and love expressed by ordinary kiwis throughout the country. The popular media was full of voices calling for more compassion, and more kindness, and none more so that our Prime Minister.

> We each hold the power, in our words and in our actions, in our daily acts of kindness. We are not immune to the viruses of hate, of fear, of other. We never have been. But we can be the nation that discovers the cure.[1]

My goal in writing this book is to reflect on how connection between ordinary people can be part of the cure. That creating and building on connections and friendships could be part of an enduring response that supports survivors to rebuild their lives, and changes society for the better. Friendship is something ordinary kiwis like us can do to build bonds of peace with survivors – many of whom are immigrants.

Here at South West Baptist Church, we have been on a journey of discovery about what it means to build communities of faith while living in a modern secular society, and what the practical application of that is. All through our history there has been a desire to build strong communities where people can find connection, belonging and meaning in their lives. Our earlier activities involved developing programmes and organisations for those among us that were facing crises or challenges in life. We still run many of those programmes and the organisations still exist, but it seems to us that they are not the full solution. With time and experience it became apparent that something more is needed. Something to sit alongside the professional and the programmes. Something to help each of us to support, care and walk alongside one another.

No matter how good or comprehensive the professional programmes are, people benefit from simply being in connection with other human beings, and connection is created through simple and repetitive acts of friendship. We all need friends. Trusted friends who can celebrate with us in the good times and help us through the bad times. Friendship is not a replacement for professional help – where it is needed – but it is a general antidote to the isolation that many of us experience.[2] Friendship builds both personal and corporate resilience. It seems so obvious and yet it is so powerful. Communities that are held together through bonds of friendship are safe, secure, welcoming places for the stranger, and for us.

The reflections in this book are just that – my reflections on the journey that our community has been on. I have reflected on our experiences of building bridges across cultures and found four common threads within those experiences. I offer these threads humbly for others to reflect on in their own expressions of community and care. Many readers will already be taking their own journeys of cross-cultural discovery and community building and will have made their own discoveries. I invite you to walk with us, help us, and together we can make many expressions of belonging, in many places.

We continue on our journey of discovery and understanding. On our journey we start by listening, offering to share the grief and the pain, and looking for ways to strengthen connections between ourselves and surrounding community resources. In walking alongside those of other cultures, we see the values of kindness, compassion and care emerging among us.

I need to clarify four things. First, the book is written by me about the journey of South West Baptist Church. It is not my story alone. The experiences are those of many people, drawn together with the intent of building stronger connections and community. The collective first person – we – is used to express the activities of many people that are walking with us on this journey, and the indented quotes capture their comments. They are not attributed to protect the privacy of the people involved, and any names used have been changed.

Second, the term stranger or newcomer is used to denote those who are not yet known to us. It is intended to be broader than former refugee or migrant. It recognises that many people are on a journey toward belonging, the journey can have many different stages, it is often not linear, and it is possible to be born or live in a country for many years and still feel like a stranger. The purpose of this book is to spur us to help each other along the journey from stranger to friend and, together to create a sense and a place of belonging.

Finally, to clarify the structure of this book. The next section reflects on recent experiences of South West Baptist Church. Four specific learnings form the basis for each of the sections following. Throughout the book are ideas and suggestions drawn from what we have learnt and recorded in the Signposts. The last section addresses some of the challenges that we have faced along the way.

The South West Baptist Church Journey

Brothers and sisters let us not forget!
We're a pilgrim church, a church on a journey.
The love of Jesus brings us to life,
as the Spirit moves and speaks to us.
We look to God, and God calls us to love our neighbour.
We look around us, and we see God bringing new life,
in our homes, in our communities and in the world.
So, we walk in hope,
joining those who celebrate and those in pain.
Because whatever we do for the least, we do for Jesus.[3]

Neighbourhood Community

South West Baptist Church has long been interested and involved in building connections and building community. In recent years, we have been thinking about the importance of the place in which we live as an integral part of creating connection. We can see place as simply the location of our house from which we live our lives, or we can see it as a fundamental part in the challenge of creating collective belonging. Māori call it tūrangawaewae: the place where one belongs because of relationship.[4]

An active appreciation of place is an important ingredient in creating belonging and connection, which in turn supports identity and encourages stewardship. Including a sense and commitment to a place reinforces the building of connections leading to enduring friendships, which in turn leads to a stronger sense of belonging – to the place and to each other. It creates opportunity to welcome others to that place.

A place perspective taps into the benefit of proximity. Living nearby to each other strengthens relationships as it makes it easier to connect both intentionally and in unplanned organic ways. Simple everyday activities of heading to work or to school, local recreation, or visiting the local shops become imbued with the possibility of connection and relationship. We can find ways to weave our lives together as a way of supporting each other.

Figure 1 Four critical relationships

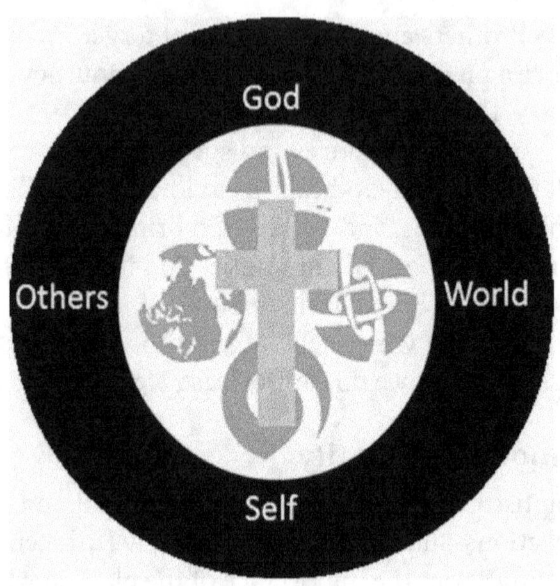

At South West Baptist we have invited people to view the places in which they live from this perspective. We have encouraged them to build their connections with others living in the same area, within a framework of four key relationships – with themselves and with God, with each other and with the world (see Figure 1). This approach can be called place-based intentional community. The word 'place,' because it is centred on where people live. The word 'intentional' because it requires effort to see our neighbours, our streets, our suburbs, and our city differently. We look to discover, and then to add to the existing layers and networks of connections and friendships in a place as a way to create a sense of belonging for everyone.

Our model of place-based intentional community is called Neighbourhood Community and we have developed eight of them in the south western suburbs of Christchurch. People in these communities see each other as co-workers in the goal of building stronger community, for collective benefit. They look for ways to weave their lives together with and for each other to encourage belonging for all who live in that area. Together they invest time and energy into their local area to foster individual growth and development and community resilience through connection and friendship.

Individual circumstances shape the expression of intentional community, so our Neighbourhood Communities are all different. But we believe – and our experience shows – that opportunities for connection can be found everywhere, and that even the smallest connection with another person in a shared place can support feelings of belonging.

Refugee Sponsorship

Across the winter of 2015, New Zealanders watched as millions of refugees fled persecution, escaping the brutal war in Syria. We joined the voices of many to petition the government to extend a welcome to additional refugees.[5] Over time and with the collective efforts of many asking our government to respond, the refugee quota was increased and a complementary pathway for former refugees to resettle in New Zealand was announced. Known as the Community Organisation Refugee Sponsorship (CORS) Category, the pilot partnered government with community organisations to help 23 refugees from the Middle East to settle in New Zealand.[6] Four organisations, including South West Baptist Church, were approved to be community sponsors in December 2017.

The sponsorship pilot is similar to a programme that has been operating in Canada for several decades.[7] New Zealand joined Ireland and the United Kingdom in setting up pilots and other countries are being invited to follow. Community sponsorship is part of a range of actions on behalf of the international community to address the escalating refugee crisis.[8] At the time of writing there are 25 million refugees and less than 100,000 government funded resettlement places world-wide.[9]

While there are unique differences between the community sponsorship programmes in different countries, at their core they engage and invite community groups (for example churches, sports clubs, professional groups) to receive and welcome refugees. In the New Zealand programme, sponsors have a two-year agreement to assist refugees to integrate into our country. Kiwis walk with them every step of the way, assisting them into housing, enrolling children into schools, and health care, and training, and providing emotional support. Set-up costs, including flights from the Mangere Refugee Centre are met by the sponsor and the refugees receive welfare as permanent residents of New Zealand.

Six refugee families came to New Zealand in mid-2018 through the pilot programme with three being welcomed by our church in Christchurch. We asked three Neighbourhood Communities to invite a former refugee family into their midst (see Figure 2). Two teams of supporters were created: people in the Neighbourhood Communities who were intentionally building trust relationships with the former refugees, and a second team in a supportive and advisory role for the first (the 'Settlement Advisory Team'). The first group appointed a coordinator (termed a Lead) whose responsibility it was to coordinate activities and work with the Church Resettlement Coordinator to make sure we fulfilled the requirements of the sponsorship agreement. Each role in the team had two people assigned to it. This was done to make sure that nothing was missed, and to give people a shared task. By assigning roles in this way we hoped to avoid overwhelming the refugee family with many people, or conversely overwhelming sponsor volunteers, while offering the potential for natural friendships to develop. A brief word of explanation on the roles: collectively they address the range of settlement activities that are required. The 'Buddy' role recognises the family as individuals within a family unit, and that each person could have different needs for support. The idea of a buddy was to have people who were engaging with the former refugees about the needs of individuals and identifying opportunities for support. Support could take the form of referrals for counselling, or additional support for children in schools.

We called our approach 'Care + Connect.' Caring for the newcomer by connecting them into the markers of successful integration (like schooling, health care, education, training and employment) in a way that infuses all these activities with relationship and a strong sense of place. We found that the way we went about these activities could foster a sense of belonging. For example, we did orientation to the area in the area, not in a classroom. We took the newcomers on walking and cycling tours in their immediate neighbourhood, showing them easy and repeatable trips to schools, shops, health and recreation centres. We took bus trips with them, taking them to the centre of Christchurch, and to halal food stores. We pointed out landmarks and shared with them our sense of belonging. The goal was to provide security and stability from which they could spring-board into independence and a life of their choosing in this new country.

Figure 2 The structure of our support

Our belief in the importance of place heavily influenced our search for houses. Our sponsorship agreement required us to find a house for each family and furnish it ready for the family to move into on arrival to Christchurch. We looked for and found houses that were located right in the midst of each Neighbourhood Community. One house was owned by a private individual not associated with our church community who upon hearing that we were asking on behalf of a refugee family, was willing to provide the house in the absence of references or before even meeting them. We were very appreciative of their willingness to do this. Another house was purchased by an individual for this specific need.[10]

We set up an inventory of household effects and invited donations. Much stuff came from people downsizing the family home. Knowing little about the incoming family and nothing about their personal interests, nor having the houses available before we began collecting meant we had several challenges in what to collect. Should we take gardening equipment? Should we accept a spinning wheel and sewing machine? Children's games? Books? Generally, we stuck to the basics, taking additional stuff only if it was excellent quality, and relying on cash donations to purchase books and games rather than taking stuff we were not at all sure would be wanted. We invited a team of people with trailers and trucks to collect household effects, storing them in containers behind the church. Just prior to arrival, supporters came together one Saturday, emptying all the containers and filling the houses with gear and getting them ready to welcome the newcomers.

In the weeks and months following arrival people started getting to know one another over meals and everyday activities like doing the grocery shopping. We invited Ngāi Tahu to join with us in a powhiri welcoming the new arrivals after they had been here for some months. We hoped that these activities, formal and otherwise, would assist the former refugees to see this place as theirs, and settle more easily through the friendships they were developing. It is apparent that this is happening.[11]

As news spread across the City of the impending arrival of refugees, we were approached by others from outside our circle of connections who were keen to lend a hand. Individuals and groups with knowledge and experience of settling refugees, former refugees and adherents of the Islamic faith helped us understand what to expect. They explained potential cultural and religious differences and helped us understand how to offer our support in the most useful ways. Practical support came from businesses offering storage containers, clothes, bicycles, computers, and more. Everywhere we turned we found ordinary kiwis wanting to help welcome the newcomers.

The March 15 Terror Attacks

The events of March 15 directly impacted all of us. The men of two of the families we had sponsored were in one of the mosques that day. A father and his seventeen-year-old son were killed. His thirteen-year-old son was badly injured. The father of the second family was also badly injured. The families were devastated and so were we. The events shattered perceptions of the safety and security of this country amidst a realisation for them, and for us, that New Zealand was not immune to hate crimes of such magnitude.

At the time of the tragic events, the three former refugee families were well into their journey of settling here. Despite having been in the country for less than 12 months, each father had part-time work. Everyone was improving their English, and children were in school. Families were financially independent of us, knew their way around the city, and were making connections among us and others in the wider community. It was early days, but it felt like they were developing a sense of belonging in this place despite the inevitable challenges and obstacles of starting again in a new country.

For our part we mourned the loss of new friends and struggled to work out how to support the survivors in culturally appropriate ways. In the immediate aftermath of the attacks, we rallied to support each family with practical and emotional needs. We responded with what we knew: that these attacks were on our friends and they needed help.

In the immediate days and weeks after the attacks we sat in on many meetings with survivor representatives, Christchurch City Council and other groups. We listened to briefings of the work that had begun to help the survivors cope with the devastating loss. We wanted to contribute but as a church we knew we were not trauma specialists, nor experts in Muslim sensibilities and needs, nor professionals (though many individuals in the congregation are). What we were, however, were people in relationships: brothers, sisters, uncles, aunties, children and parents and grandparents. We knew something of the value of relationships. We were friends and neighbours of survivors. We lived in this city, we belonged, and we were safe, and we wanted to help restore those feelings for others. We wanted to support survivors to rebuild their lives and gain a sense of security, safety and hope.

In listening to the discourse and dialogue in and around Christchurch in the aftermath, it seemed to us that responses to the terror attacks could be seen as either professional in nature to address a specific issue, or an intervention designed to build connections with others. It was the latter that we felt we could support, through intentional and enduring friendship.

We started by talking to the survivors with whom we already had a connection: the sponsored families, and others whom we knew who had been caught up in the attacks. Our intent in starting and building on existing connections was to come as friends: to sit and to listen and to try to understand. With understanding came an awareness of needs to which we could respond. We did not seek to take the place of experts and professionals. Nor did we attempt to meet every need from our own resources. We saw ourselves for who we were: people in the neighbourhood, in the house next door, at the same workplace, so what we offered was something natural, yet which needed to be intentional. We came together to offer simple friendship.

Writing this now it is hard to believe that something as simple as friendship could make a meaningful difference. And yet we think it does. As connections and friendships developed, we began to hear hints of the meaningfulness that friendship offered:

> As I sat listening to Mohammed speak, I had again such a sense
> of the loss that they have experienced. Loss of home, of country,
> of friendships, of history and of culture. What can I say in the
> face of this loss? But when I left an hour and a half and a cup of
> tea later, they said how thankful they were for the friends that
> they had made.

Building connection and friendship with people of different cultural and religious understandings is slow and incremental, but we are building something enduring. Sometimes sitting together has moved onto supporting practical care. Some of our activity has been in supporting community events organised by others or aiding the survivors in their own efforts to provide for themselves and others. But more often the work is with individuals and families, in homes, in small and fleeting and seemingly unimportant ways. Often it is about simply making time and space in our day to match their willingness to reach out and befriend.

There seemed to be a change about three months after the terror attacks. Daily practical needs gave way to requests for assistance with visas as survivors applied for extended family to come to New Zealand to support them. While not being experts in immigration law, we could nonetheless help with preparation of forms, and finding lawyers who could help. With the passing of the most urgent needs, survivors started to contemplate a different future, and friendship seemed to take on new meaning and value.

For us at South West Baptist it became an opportunity to reflect on the tumultuous few months since the terror attacks and our experiences of offering friendship. We reflected on the value of intentional connection and friendship to see if there was anything that might form part of a more enduring response, both for survivors of the attacks and for ourselves in making the City a safer and more welcoming place. We thought about what we had learnt about how to build bridges across the chasms that divide people of different cultural and religious understandings. From those reflections we saw four common threads that were woven through all our experiences which are helpful to think about in welcoming the stranger and building bridges with people of difference in our midst.

Common Threads

The four overlapping threads weaving through all our experiences offer hints or signposts towards building friendships between people of different cultures, religions and backgrounds.

The first thread is to be clear about intentions and values. Being clear about these factors requires us to consider some big questions like: What motivates us? Why are we doing this? How committed are we? What can we offer, and for how long? Being explicit about our core values and our intentions helps us navigate the inevitable questions that come up and shapes the interactions we have. We have identified three bedrock values that have been critical for us – authenticity, humility and empowerment.

The second thread is to gather a bunch of committed people to extend a hand of friendship together. Recognising that although friendship is a simple and natural activity, sometimes it requires us to go out of our way or do something different. As individuals it is a challenging thing to embark on because it takes time that we may not always feel that we have. Building intentional friendships alongside and with others helps us to celebrate our intriguing and interesting differences, and to cope with the confronting and confusing ones. Building enduring relationships between people of different cultural backgrounds can be challenging, so having a group of people to do it with not only makes it more fun but helps us navigate rocky waters. The other benefit of doing it together is that it gives a stranger access through us to an existing network of connections. Initially this assists with friendship and a developing sense of belonging, and in time it can help with employment.

The third thread is to think about the places we inhabit and interact. Most of our lives occupy the same places as we move through our regular routines. Living near to the people we are trying to connect with makes it easier to maintain the commitment of authentic friendship. Living in proximity of place supports planned interaction but also allows for accidental interaction as we 'bump' into each other as we move about in our daily lives. For example, recently I bumped into a new friend at the local recreation centre. Encounters like this are seemingly insignificant on their own but when repeated and combined with other interactions create connection. All these connections when layered on top of one another create a sense of belonging to a place.

The final thread is knowledge. Having even a little knowledge about the culture or religion of the people we are befriending demonstrates and earns respect and creates trust. Knowing a few words of a language or some of the key cultural traditions around the home can avoid offence in the early stages of relationship-building.

Knowledge includes self-awareness, which also feeds back into values. For example, talking about our motivations with our team can help us figure out what empowerment looks like for us and for those we are befriending. Challenging our conscious and unconscious attitudes helps us to grow and helps us to avoid offending or hurting those we are trying to welcome. We all bring cultural and experiential blinkers to all that we do, often without realising this. We need people who can give us honest advice and we need to be humble and willing to learn.

Thread 1: Foundational Values

Foundational values are the why of actions. These values underpin and permeate every action, every thought. They can be explicit and known to us or hidden in our unconscious. Examining our values at the outset is of fundamental importance because it helps us to understand what motivates us.

Values provide a touchstone to return to, when faced with challenges and to figure out the way forward. They help you stay focused and committed because you know why you're doing this stuff, and why you're doing it together.

In the goal of welcoming newcomers to settle into our city, and in responding to the terror attacks, we have returned time and again to three key values that have really helped guide us: authenticity, humility and empowerment.

Authenticity

Authentic friendship is friendship without strings or ulterior motives. If the goal is friendship for a purpose other than knowing and being known, then friendship loses authenticity, and becomes false. Intentional friendship can cause issues if there is confusion about the intent. Friendship is authentic when it comes from a desire to create a sense of belonging together and wanting what is best for the other.

Authentic friendship is more than friendliness. Kiwis are naturally friendly. We acknowledge one another. We smile and wave. Sometimes we say hello. But friendship goes deeper to intentionally draw others into our lives and our connections. Newcomers report a lack of friendship with New Zealand-born people.[12] Building friendships, particularly across cross-cultural divides requires more than friendliness. Authentic friendship goes further, into a willingness to invest time into friendship:

> It's not something you can fail at, because these are people's
> lives, not something we can walk away from after 6 months.
> Relationships are long-term, even though the initial
> [sponsorship] commitment is for two years, it is a lifetime
> relationship that we are building, because they're our friends; it's
> not going to end just because time has passed.

The value of being a friend should not be underestimated. Someone to laugh with, someone to navigate life with. Someone who cares enough to invest time and energy in the relationship. But consistency in the friendship is key to building trust:

> Figure out what you can offer and stick with that. If you
> go around once a week, go around once a week. But don't
> spend a lot of time over a short period and then not see
> them for the next month. This is confusing and can lead to
> misunderstandings.

Authentic friendship is a two-way street, moving away from 'us' and 'them' towards 'together, we'. We listen to understand and through this we learn and change. Authentic relationships take time to build through listening to the life of another person with a genuine heart. Using active listening[13] helps us to concentrate on what is being said so we can understand, respond to, and respect and remember what has been shared with us.

Humility

The concept of humility is both a frame of mind and a way of acting. Being humble requires a conscious decision to seek to understand before responding, and to look past those things that might otherwise offend. Being humble means giving and receiving with no expectation of or need for reciprocation.

Adopting humility as a key value reminds us that there are at least two world views in play. Remembering that welcoming another person involves the intersection of cultures with their attendant similarities and differences. It means that we expect that there will be times when we misunderstand each other:

> I knew the offer was made in kindness and I also knew that
> Mohammed would have been paid to do this in his country
> because he had told me. It was a tricky situation but when both
> perspectives were explained we all had a good laugh about it.

Friendship requires trust, and trust takes time to develop. In the early days of connecting a desire to befriend can be misconstrued or misunderstood. Time and consistency will address this. An attitude of humility does not say we will accept everything or do everything asked of us. But humility does say that we will work hard to understand before acting:

> We knew enough of their culture to know that they would not
> express gratitude the way we're used to. Even so, it was pretty
> hard to hear their anger and frustration that we would not do
> what they wanted, with not one word of thanks for what we had
> done.

Humility does not pander nor excuse. It does not condone nasty behaviour. It does not accept abuse or aggression. But humility works hard to avoid assumptions. Being humble is about stepping into someone else's shoes, to see their perspective, and to look through and beyond conflict situations to see and understand the person.

Humility means accepting that we can learn from other perspectives. Recognising that our best efforts might not be enough if we fail to identify and reflect on our biases and preconceptions. We know that we are likely to make mistakes however well-intentioned we are, and that we must work hard to avoid mistakes that could be harmful. Being humble knows that we need to hear the stories of newcomers to understand how welcoming kiwis really are:

> I was surprised to hear how he had been treated in New Zealand
> since he had arrived as a refugee. How he had been told he
> should be grateful that New Zealand had allowed him to come
> here. How long was he meant to be grateful? His whole life?

Empowerment

Empowerment is the idea that we are helping someone else to achieve their hopes, dreams and goals. More formally it could be described as strengthening and building confidence in people to make their own decisions and to take control of their own lives. Empowerment is a bedrock value for South West Baptist because we don't want to create dependency nor impose a perspective on how others should live. Instead we want newcomers to thrive in the ways they want to.

Adopting a value of empowerment encourages conversations around the long-term implications of our actions, whether these are to assist a newcomer to settle, or to build a friendship with a stranger. It is an important value to reflect on because it can be difficult to apply. Sometimes actions that mean well are misguided, and it is better to discover this beforehand. Thinking hard about what empowerment looks like and what our motivations are helps us understand who benefits from the intended action: we may discover it meets our needs more than those we seek to befriend.

Lending a hand is a typical kiwi characteristic. The problem arises if that 'help' emphasises our power and reduces the recipients learning opportunity to do it for themselves. I am not saying we don't help people. Quite the reverse. What I am saying is that actions should be considered through the lens of empowerment.

At the core of every action we have taken has been a commitment to empowerment. There are some things that we had to prepare for the former refugees before they arrived. For example, we had to find and furnish houses. We asked people of similar background what would be important in a house. But true empowerment would have invited the former refugee family to have made their own decisions about where and how they would live. As much as possible we have tried to help strangers to navigate life in Christchurch and allow them to make their own decisions independently of us. Sometimes this meant actions as simple as thinking about how to get somewhere:

> Giving [someone] a lift seems like the obvious thing to do – but
> if it is a journey that the family will want to repeat, then think
> about teaching them how the bus system works.

Empowerment also means respecting their decisions, even if we disagree. We work on the principle of helping, not doing. This could mean listening to a request, helping to find relevant information, helping to weigh up a decision, or exploring together the implications of a decision. Sometimes it's frustrating – for both parties – but ultimately it should lead to better outcomes. Imposing our will through making decisions for others takes away power, even if there is a seemingly positive outcome. Supporting their decision, even if we disagree, ultimately leads to better long-term outcomes.

Sometimes the implications of our actions are unclear. Sometimes the line between 'doing with' and 'doing for' is fuzzy. In the initial days of resettlement, and again after the terror attacks, we did things for our friends. We became more protective in our actions. We anticipated their daily needs and offered practical support to meet them. We made halal meals. Drove people from home to hospital to morgue and back again. Mowed the lawns. Cleared the letterbox. Took family to funerals. We knew these actions were not empowering, but we also recognised it was appropriate for a time and a place, but not permanently. Without a bedrock value of empowerment, these good intentions could have morphed into creating dependency and become unhelpful:

> At first, I would pick up their child from school and take them to their sports practice, but it was only a 10-minute walk for them, so they now do this.

Empowerment recognises that our hopes for another's life must necessarily be secondary to their hopes. With that always at the front of our minds, we must consider our actions carefully.

Signposts

Identify the values that are important to you. How do they play out in real life? Consider different scenarios and identify behaviours that reflect your values. Identify those behaviours that are not based on your values. Tease out your motivations. Think about your reactions to an uncomfortable situation before it happens.

Examine your motives in friendship. Friendship for its own sake, or for the sake of the other is powerful and life-changing.

Be consistently, not constantly available, at whatever level of interaction you can sustain. Building friendship takes time. Give yourself and others' time. Value your contribution, however small it seems.

Listen.

Don't underestimate the power of connection, or the importance of being a friend.

Find a connection point, something you have in common that you are naturally drawn to, whether that be a shared love of cooking, or recreation, or being a parent.

Be kind to yourselves and others. Mistakes will be made. An attitude of humility gives and receives forgiveness – to yourself and to others. People are generally forgiving, especially if you approach them with humility and a willingness to learn.

Think hard about how to empower others. Resist the urge to provide a response for the immediate situation without thinking of the bigger picture. Instead, work in ways that build confidence and capability.

Empowering others means to place them at the centre of whatever must be done. Wherever possible explain what needs to be done to the newcomer and get their perspectives on how they would like to be supported.

For example, invite the newcomer to choose their bank, internet provider or doctor. Show them how to do things rather than doing things for them. Throw light on the hidden cultural norms in our society and the way things work here. For example, that we must be proactive in dealing with government departments and that police are not corrupt and can be approached in the street for help. Show them how to find useful information and support them in making their decisions.

Ask yourself: is this something I will happily do repeatedly? If not, think about how to teach them to do it themselves. A common example is transport. Teach newcomers to use the bus rather than take them everywhere in your car. Using your car seems such an obvious and helpful thing to do, but what happens when you are not available? How will they get around?

Thread 2: Extend the Hand of Friendship Together

Our Neighbourhood Communities consisted of people who already knew each other, with many of them living near each other, and whose lives were already interwoven to some extent. These existing connections aided cross-cultural relationship building because newcomers were drawn into the existing layers of connection. For example, a bunch of guys included a newcomer for some practical house renovation followed by a family barbeque. A kiwi family and a newcomer family got together to stack their firewood for the winter. In both situations people doing something together for mutual benefit created a sense of togetherness and natural opportunities for conversation and easy interaction.

Building friendships between people of different cultural background can take time and requires a commitment to be consistent. Having a team of people that collectively agree to extend a hand of friendship makes it easier. Having a range of different people on the journey together creates opportunities for natural friendships to emerge and offers different perspectives on how to progress. It also shares the load when prior commitments absorb our time.

Building a team involves gathering a group of people who are prepared to invest some of their time and learn. In the resettlement journey the sponsorship agreement set out what was needed, and we chose to apply a semi-formal approach with assigned roles (see Figure 2). This approach is not applicable to building bridges with people of difference who have lived in New Zealand for some time. However, having a team approach is still useful because of the challenges inherent in developing authentic and long-lasting relationships of trust.

Developing a team with diverse skills supports effective integration of the stranger. These diverse skills could be anything from preparing food to understanding the New Zealand tax system, through to having time in the day to be present to sit, and to listen. These skills are all valuable in the goal of helping the stranger to a place of belonging:

> Some sponsor teams were already established with good foundational relationships. This made it easier to tune into what people are good at. Because the team all agreed that they were going to fully commit the time needed, people stepped up when needed, and tasks were easily delegated to the most suitable person. Some people were not able to commit as much time due to their own circumstances but could contribute in different ways.

Having a team of people who have some level of existing relationships with each other can be helpful. Teams must be internally supportive – with people willing to help each other. As difficult conversations or challenges arise, your team must have some resilience – an untapped capacity to draw from – and a safe space in which to unpack together what individuals are feeling and experiencing. The commitment to existing relationships pulls together and brings benefits for the stranger and for each other. Without a team of committed individuals, the work of building trust can fall on a few which is hard to sustain over the long-term:

> Most people got involved in sponsoring because they knew the newcomer would need help in all sorts of ways. Realising that I alone can't do this and reaching out to others is important. And then knowing how to make your help work with others' help.

A healthy team environment should challenge individual values, attitudes and unconscious biases. For example, how do we react when we see a woman wearing a head-scarf? Talking together can identify unhelpful attitudes that will stifle or prevent flourishing of cross-cultural relationships. Permission to talk within a committed and safe environment can assist the group to see the value brought by each individual and how that might be harnessed for collective and individual good. Learning to listen in humility can be hugely transformational and bring a team together:

> You have to be willing to put yourself out of your comfort zone
> and talk with people who don't speak very much English. You
> have to learn how to be a guest and accept hospitality as well as
> give it. Your role is as a gracious guest, not to come with answers
> and solutions, tempting though that is. It takes humility. There
> is a lot about friendship that is simply being there. Being present
> and making time for people is very important.

We all have connections into the world around us. Combining our connections with others in the team can create bridges for a stranger to enter our world. Each of our connections can lead to other connections. If we think of our networks as opportunities that can be harnessed for the good of someone else, they can become quite powerful. Our experience has been that as we come together, we can find connections to assist the stranger move toward belonging. We have discovered that among our combined network of connections are people willing to contribute to the goal of creating belonging. Often our role is simply to connect and to show others how they might meaningfully offer support and initiate relationship.

Being visible in your friendship with strangers can reduce the barriers to others taking the first step toward relationship. One of our team was walking to playcentre with one of the former refugees when a third woman approached them. Our team member told me later:

> The woman who came up to us and started talking was someone
> I knew a little. I think she felt more comfortable talking to Sara
> because I was obviously comfortable in being with her. I doubt
> she would have approached a woman wearing a hijab otherwise.

Sometimes simply being with a stranger sends a powerful message to others about how they can act to make connections.

Signposts

Develop collective values and expected behaviours for your team. Here are the values that were developed for our support for former refugees.

We have identified these values that underpin our place-based Care + Connect approach:

- Our goal is to support refugees to become fully functioning members of society, in a way that is respectful of their beliefs and culture. We will not force our beliefs or religious views upon them.

- We are partnering with the former refugees and the government to achieve the goal of self-sufficiency. Partners act in good faith toward each other and on an equal footing.

- We will endeavour to provide the former refugees with choice and support them to make their own decisions about life, even when we disagree with their decisions.

- We accept that there will be times and situations where the former refugees do not react in ways that we might expect.

- Part of supporting them to make new lives for themselves is in the language we use. We will refer to them in language that does not betray their history. We will maintain their privacy better than we would our own, only discuss their needs in respect of completing this project, and not otherwise talk about them to third parties unless they are comfortable that we are doing so.

- We will care for each other and set healthy rhythms for ourselves and each other.

- We will endeavour to be open with each other about how things are going, and we will avail ourselves of the networks of care that surround us.

We ask that as a group supporting former refugees to settle you:

- Work with the church and the former refugees to support them to become self-sufficient by mid-2020.

- Accept other faiths and cultures, including being supportive of the right of others to maintain their faith and culture.

- Commit to being a cohesive group with an existing structure in place.

- Offer relevant experience of working with vulnerable people of different cultural and religious backgrounds.

- Are sufficiently diverse as a group to identify with and support strangers to our place.

Creating teams of people of different ages, life stages and skills is helpful. Diversity creates different opportunities for friendship. Having men, women and children willing to be friends, respects cultural sensitivities and creates opportunities for natural friendships to form.

Invite people of similar cultural backgrounds to participate and provide advice.

Having fun times together creates opportunities for friendships to form, with each other and with the newcomers.

Assign roles for people and discuss expectations. Team members need to have a clear understanding of their role and what needs to be communicated with each other. Establishing guidelines and expectations is important for building a sense of shared purpose. Have one or two people in a coordination role to provide structure and purpose, raise issues for group discussion and be a contact person for other agencies. Remember: the wider the support network, the wider the skill base, but also the more time-consuming to coordinate.

Regular face to face communication in the team supports having a common purpose and avoids over-reliance on electronic communications that can go astray. Meetings were supported by WhatsApp which is ideally suited for practical daily communication.

Be respectful with shared information and maintain privacy of the newcomers.

Consider nominating a coordinator. Rely on the coordinator for difficult conversations, for example about the financial support that the group can give. Doing this avoids threatening relationships, particularly in the early days, and allows those closest to the newcomers to concentrate on forming friendships.

Think about the collective network of connections that your team has. Identify the opportunities that may exist and who could be invited to assist with supporting a stranger develop a sense of belonging. Recognise that as an established person in New Zealand you have much to offer a newcomer.

Thread 3: Think Differently About Place

Our lives are embedded in places. We live, work, play, visit friends and socialise in places: often in places close to each other. Take my life for example: I live at the base of the Port Hills, Christchurch. I cycle five kilometres to work along the Heathcote River. My children bike or walk to the local school, and I exercise locally: running or biking in the hills and walking the dog through the streets in my neighbourhood. Most of my life takes place within ten kilometres of my house. The same can be said for most of us. The majority of our lives are or can be lived locally.

We can view our places as simply areas to pass through as we go about our daily routines, or we can see them as places rich in opportunity for building connections. If we take the latter perspective, then our daily routines take on new meaning as we look for opportunities to build connection with others that share our place. Our places can then become infused with connections and relationships, deepening our sense of belonging and security as we develop ownership and stewardship for our place.

My place is sandwiched between the Port Hills and the Heathcote River. I know I'm in my place when I see hills in three directions. There is the house on the street that used to belong to the Scotsman and now there is a young family in it. The playcentre I took my children to now has Sikh services on an evening and the street comes alive with splendidly dressed women and men with turbans piled high on their heads. If we look carefully, we will find that there are people of difference sharing our places. There are people who may have experienced a sense of disconnection or isolation or who are survivors of the terror attacks. Through our actions in our place we can offer something tangible that is a step towards creating connection and a sense of shared belonging and security.

In welcoming refugees to Christchurch and in connecting with survivors of the terror attacks, we have harnessed the power of place to assist in creating a sense of belonging. Let me give you an example. Every house we found for the newcomers is in proximity to the local people that volunteered to support and befriend them. Each family lives in the centre of a web of existing friendships and relationships between people who are actively looking out for them. Together they find ways for connection and integration, whether that be through planned activities such as shared meals or through accidental interaction.

Our first steps in attempting to support survivors of the terror attacks were to find them in the places where we lived and worked, and then to look for ways to make connections. From there came invitations to sit and to listen and then, and only then, to offer the help and support they wanted.

A focus on place makes connecting with others more natural, more stable, and more likely to succeed over time. Making friends and spending time together is much easier if people live in near proximity. Proximity also supports planned interactions because it is easier to visit someone if they live on our way to somewhere else. Having to go out of our way creates another thing to do in a busy day and can reduce the likelihood of it becoming a regular occurrence.

Living near to each other reduces dependence on cars (newcomers often do not have licenses or cars) and supports other forms of transport. Proximity supports connection at many ages: adults with each other, for example, or children meeting in the local park. Proximity fosters interaction which in turn fosters belonging.

Proximity of place also creates opportunity for unplanned interaction. There is a strand of city planning called place-making, and reference is made to 'bumping spaces' – spaces that are natural intersection points where people meet up simply going about their daily business: taking children to school, going to the local shops.[14] Proximity also creates opportunities for children to connect, for example on their way to school or in the local park after school.

Living in proximity has meant that children of new and established families often attend the same schools and have been able to look out for one another. This proximity of place eases the challenge and increases our ability to meet the needs presented, as well as creating opportunities for friendships and connection to naturally develop as we all go about our daily lives.

Signposts

Think about your daily life as a place where you can meet and welcome the stranger. With your team map your neighbourhood.

- Where do you all live?

- What are the pathways you take as you move through your regular routines?

- Where do those paths intersect?

- What are the common interaction points? Where are the places that people congregate?

- Can you adjust your daily schedule to linger in those places to build on a connection?

Look for those people of difference in your lives, and act to engage with them. Start with eye contact or a smile of acknowledgement.

Create time in your daily routine for interactions with people.

Consider changing the way you move about. Replace car trips with cycling, walking or catching the bus because cars create barriers to human interaction.

Thread 4: Knowledge

Gaining knowledge is vital to avoiding harmful mistakes and to do the best we can in making connections. Two key parts to befriending people of other cultural background are:

- to understand something of the culture, values and perspectives of the people you are building bridges with, and

- to understand your own culture, beliefs and biases.

There is a tension between believing we cannot assist unless we are an 'expert' and falling into the trap that suggests that building connection through friendship is natural and therefore we do not need to learn anything. Neither attitude is correct. We must be open to learning – about ourselves, about other cultures, and about the newcomer experience – so that our hands of friendship are extended in the best way possible: the way that is most likely to be received well.

Reflecting on our own, as well as others' cultures, helps us to learn to see things from different perspectives. While learning about another culture, reflect on your own culture and the way you were brought up, and how that creates a bias in the way you view the world. Building cross-cultural relationships is about being aware of our biases and bridging our differences by focusing on the things that unite us. For example, we all want safe and secure places to live and enjoy with friends and with family.

Building cross-cultural relationships promotes a greater understanding of different cultures and religious groups. Only through this greater understanding can we bridge and bond with others to create a mutual sense of belonging. However, keep in mind that culture is just one of the many aspects that inform how people live and behave. Factors such as age, gender, personality, or differences in upbringing will influence the way culture is expressed.

Knowledge of another culture takes research and experience. There are people already living in New Zealand who will have had similar experiences to those whom we wish to befriend, and who can offer us advice and assistance. Our experience was that they were only too willing to teach us. They helped us to see those hidden things that we all take for granted but which can be bewildering for a newcomer.

While learning about another culture it is important to avoid assumptions or generalisations. Like assuming that Australians are the same as Kiwis! It is also unreasonable to expect one person to represent their entire ethnic group, culture, religion, or race. It is helpful to learn about the general culture but don't make assumptions about the individual. Ask sincere questions and listen to what people say without judgment. Building bridges is about creating trust and respect which may start with looking for the things we have in common. In time you can recognise and celebrate the differences. Suspend judgement of others' world view. As much as we might find other cultures perplexing, there will be aspects of our culture that seem strange to people who have not grown up here.

Sharing food together can be a good basis for getting to know one another. Food is great for relaxing everyone and to let conversations flow more freely. But be aware of cultural norms. For example, be ready to explain what a pot-luck dinner is, or what it means to bring a plate.

Awareness of key cultural events like Ramadan[15] can create opportunities for further interaction. We created Ramadan care packs of dates, Turkish delight and flat bread with the advice of a local halal butcher. We offered them for when the fast was broken at the end of each day. They were received well and created opportunities for connection and conversation and demonstrated commitment to greater understanding and relationship.

Learning about the refugee experience is also invaluable. We were greatly influenced by hearing from former refugee children who had come to New Zealand many years prior. Without exception, they talked about feeling isolated and the associated mental health impacts. Another common theme was about being bullied, and at the same time feeling the pressure of academic success as families who had lost so much, placed hopes and dreams on their shoulders. They shared a sense of being alone: of not having adults other than parents to help them make sense of a world where they were the educated integrated one among a family still applying cultural hierarchical norms. As one young woman described it:

> I was the lion and the mouse. I had to speak for the family outside but in the house, I was the respectful child, supposed to be guided by my parents.

Signposts

Learn about the person's culture. Any effort will go a long way in showing that you care enough to find out about the reality of another person's life. Talk and ask questions, go to a cultural event, read books, search the internet, but know that this is simply a start and that we have much to learn as well as teach.

Engage with others' and take advice. Be ready to invite the stranger to connect with people of similar background and cultural perspective.

Make opportunities to learn, but do not let a lack of knowledge stop you from extending a hand of friendship.

Get advice from former refugees and migrants who can help you understand what it is like to come to New Zealand.

Remember that anything we learn about the culture of the newcomer will not automatically apply to that individual, in the same way that not all kiwis are into rugby, racing and beer.

Invest time into knowing yourself and your team. Make safe spaces for your team to identify and share their unconscious biases, prejudices and fears. Examine your own cultural biases. Be willing to acknowledge that your way is not the only way to do things. Be open minded, humble and willing to learn. Be forgiving of your and others' mistakes.

Find opportunities to do things together. Actions speak louder than words. Doing things together creates opportunities for natural friendship to flourish.

When Threads Unravel

In the previous sections I focus on the benefits of having clear values, working together and learning, but sometimes these threads are in danger of unravelling. Thinking about the hard issues that can arise is crucial to being ready for them. We must acknowledge that creating connection and enduring friendship between people with different experiences, upbringing, faith, and cultural background will throw up challenges and misunderstandings. These are some of the challenges we have had along the way.

Biases and expectations

Everyone has biases and expectations, although they are not always acknowledged. Working hard to identify our unconscious biases was essential to our preparation. For example, a refugee is not necessarily poor or uneducated. A refugee is someone unable to remain in their own country through fear of war, violence or persecution.[16]

We sought the advice and assistance of a trained cross-cultural facilitator to help us understand our misconceptions. We gave people in our teams' permission to express how they were feeling, and we encouraged teams to meet regularly to talk about how things were going. Through this preparation we hoped to be able to actively fight against our hidden biases and unacknowledged prejudices.

Expectations are not set agreements between people, but are beliefs, assumptions and thoughts about future outcomes or actions. It is important to identify, discuss and manage individual and group expectations, because unmet expectations can lead to feelings of frustration, anger and disappointment. As with other challenges, using values of authentic friendship, empowerment and humility are useful touchstones for developing thoughts around how to manage expectations:

> We tried to have no expectations for the family coming because
> that is an unfair way to begin. Be aware that when they come
> into the house that you have just done up, they may not like
> it done like this. You cannot take offence if you are never
> thanked for it, or if next week you see donated stuff out on the
> curb side for disposal. This is not a job for recognition, but an
> opportunity to serve and support others.

People won't always be grateful or thankful for the preparations that have been made or the effort you put in. Gratitude and outward expressions of thankfulness are not cultural norms for every culture or individual, nor should we expect them to be attached to humanitarian actions. Everyone is operating from their own cultural perspective and something of value for one can be worthless to another. Having a sense of that cultural lens helps us to better understand ourselves and others.

Friendship and Support

Our goal is to assist strangers to establish a safe and secure platform from which they can determine their own future. We recognise a power imbalance in that we are operating from a position of relative stability, wealth and embedded cultural knowledge of this place. Empowering others from our abundance of resources is challenging. It is tempting to think we must restore the newcomer to former levels of wealth, or to our socio-economic status. Navigating these issues takes care and thoughtfulness. How will you react if you are asked for money or for a favour that goes beyond what you are willing to do?

Be aware that you are in a privileged position: that you will almost certainly know more about the newcomer than they do about you. We tried to address this imbalance by creating written introductions with personal information about ourselves, and the house and neighbourhood that the family would be living in. We invited their questions and responded as best we could.

Supporters and friends must be respectful of knowledge they gain about the stranger. Personal information must be treated as private and shared only with permission of the stranger. At the same time, we must act if we observe or suspect possible harm to children or vulnerable people. Situations may arise that conflict with New Zealand law. For example, the restriction on parents hitting children.

There may be times where friends need to place limits on how they are interacting, or what they are asked to do, to make sure everyone's needs are meet. Being honest, being mindful of your values and assigning difficult conversations to a coordinator are helpful ways to work through possible issues in ways that maintain relationships.

Promoting empowerment in every situation is not always the best course of action. Situations may arise where empowering actions could lead to harm of others. For example, the use of cars. Other countries may not have such tight restrictions on requiring a license, using seatbelts or baby seats, restrictions on using a phone while driving or driving under the influence of drugs or alcohol. There may be times when intervention on the grounds of safety is needed. Think about what you might do to be respectful in such a situation.

Money

Furnishing a house and helping others to settle in New Zealand takes resources. Many times, after the March 15 terror attacks people wanted to give money. Sometimes a gift of money might seem the best way to help as it allows people to make their own decisions about what is best for them. Giving money can meet an immediate or practical need. But gifts of money can also create a charity or dependency mentality for both recipient and giver and can become an impediment to authentic friendship.

To manage this, we asked ourselves three questions before giving money:

- Would a gift of money empower the recipient?

- Would a gift of money impede the building of an authentic friendship?

- Were there other avenues to meet this need?

For us the value of empowerment was always fundamental, particularly when the relationship was new or fragile. We always looked for ways to support people to help themselves. Sometimes that meant financial gifts, but more often it meant on-going support to help people navigate society to get what they needed.

Faith conversations

Western secular views are often at odds with the views and beliefs in other parts of the world that newcomers may be coming from. Conversations about God may be welcomed by newcomers as they seek to understand their new environment and what is happening around them. The importance and support that victims of the terror attacks derived from their faith was very clear.[17] Our role in supporting newcomers must be respectful of the beliefs of others. Put yourself in their shoes and think about the importance of faith to us. How would we wish our views and beliefs to be recognised and respected?

Care must be taken to understand the individual and what they want. Respect is key. If faith conversations are to be had, then both parties must be willing to engage in the discussion. Take care in how you approach these conversations and make sure your motivation is to support, to encourage and to learn. Sharing the distinction of being people with faith in God in a secular country may be a bonding experience. Be clear that supporting others, particularly in situations of vulnerability, should not be seen as an opportunity to convert others to different beliefs. Instead, we support newcomers to practice their own religion and beliefs.

Navigating Service Providers

Working with government departments and service organisations can be daunting and confusing. Every government department must provide translation services, but this often needs to be arranged in advance. Do not assume that organisations working in similar areas will communicate with each other. Nor should you assume they will be proactive, or that they are equally understandable or available to everyone. Interaction with a service requires knowledge, some of which is hidden from those unfamiliar with the service or the culture – including ourselves.

Friends can help access a service that a stranger would not think to ask about. A friend can help, support, encourage and explain what might be needed to access the service. It is important however that friendship does not seek to replicate or replace the work of these organisations but instead supports engagement as necessary. Having someone with some knowledge of a service in your team can be invaluable in learning to navigate the system.

Signposts

Reach out for advice from people and organisations who have experience in welcoming newcomers.

Be open to and non-judgemental about other perspectives, including criticism of our country. Do not assume that 'our way' is better.

Avoid generalisations but instead speak from a personal viewpoint "I believe…"

Be respectful of other beliefs and perspectives. Ask questions and be prepared to answer questions about your beliefs.

Address any issues that arise due to miscommunication or unmet expectations to prevent the situation escalating or creating barriers to relationships.

Never assume. When in doubt, ask.

Be ready to help the newcomer engage with government and service providers.

Discovering our own biases can be uncomfortable and might need expert help to work through. Self-care is vital. Your team can help with this but there may be occasions when specialist intervention is helpful. Visit a counsellor or spiritual director. Take care of yourselves and each other.

Conclusion

This book is about reaching out and welcoming others through friendship. It offers a perspective on friendship that recognises its power to bridge differences between people of different cultural background. My hope is to stimulate conversation and debate and to show people that it may be easier than we think to build bridges with the strangers in our midst.

We all need friends. Whether we are newcomers to Aotearoa New Zealand, or we have been here for decades, friendship creates belonging and adds meaning to life. Looking to befriend is an opportunity to learn about others and ourselves. Living our lives in ways that include others in the places we inhabit can add richness and meaning for all of us.

Friendship is natural, daily, inclusive. Everyone can have and be a friend. It is a simple cure – so simple as to be in danger of being overlooked. When the media interest has died and funding runs out for the programmes and events, friendships can endure.

But while friendliness is easy, friendship between people of cultural differences can be challenging. It can be hard to initiate a connection with someone who looks, sounds and speaks differently, particularly if our lives are full of existing friendships. We may feel we do not have time. We may feel uncomfortable or intimidated. We may perceive others to have needs that will overwhelm us.

My advice is to start with small steps in your local place. Look for the people in your orbit of life and start with acknowledging their presence. Find ways to connect. Gather with others with a similar commitment to befriend. Create opportunities to meet. Map your place and find the natural intersection points and make space in your day to capture those moments of natural interaction.

Friendship as a cure seems insignificant. We might ask ourselves, as I have done many times, what value can friendship have, in the challenge of dealing with the aftermath of the terror attacks, or when welcoming a newcomer to settle in New Zealand. Through our experiences we have seen the difference that personal connection with others has had. We have been assured that it has value.

When our church started preparing for the arrival of three former refugee families from the other side of the world, I asked someone who had made a similar journey a few years previously:

What is one thing you wished you had when you arrived?

I had no idea what to expect. Perhaps a warm house, a safe place to raise children, a better way of life. I was completely unprepared for the answer:

I wish that I had had a friend.

Friendship is so simple an idea – yet offers such a difference.

Notes

1 https://thespinoff.co.nz/politics/08-04-2019/humanity-thats-all-jacinda-ardern-on-the-response-to-the-christchurch-attacks/

2 https://www.stuff.co.nz/national/health/106531307/the-isolated-ill-how-mental-illness-and-isolation-interact

3 Prayer commonly recited at South West Baptist church gatherings.

4 https://maoridictionary.co.nz

5 https://www.stuff.co.nz/the-press/71811234/churches-commit-to-housing-hundreds-of-extra-refugees

6 https://www.immigration.govt.nz/about-us/media-centre/news-notifications/community-organisation-refugee-sponsorship-category-introduced

7 https://www.canada.ca/en/immigration-refugees-citizenship/services/refugees/help-outside-canada/private-sponsorship-program.html

8 See the Global Compact on Refugees 2018 that identifies community sponsorship as one of four approaches to address the refugee crisis: https://www.unhcr.org/the-global-compact-on-refugees.html

9 https://www.unhcr.org/figures-at-a-glance

10 We have had other offers of houses, either from people that own rental houses or from others willing to purchase houses to rent to former refugees.

11 As well as our experiences, an independent government evaluation noted that the CORS pilot had successfully brought communities together and recorded the former refugees as saying that the practical and emotional support received had been very helpful. https://www.mbie.govt.nz/assets/d3cedd12c2/community-organisation-refugee-sponsorship-category-pilot-process-evaluation.pdf

12 **https://www.stuff.co.nz/travel/news/112920098/what-life-is-like-in-new-zealand-according-to-expats**

    https://www.stuff.co.nz/national/christchurch-shooting/113432617/are-kiwis-welcoming-enough-to-immigrants

13 As the name suggests, active listening means to be active in the task of listening, fully concentrating on what is being said, rather than passively listening to the conversation.

14 See for example **https://localgovernmentmag.co.nz/where-do-we-dance-planning-social-spaces-in-the-suburb/**

15 An important Islamic event during which Muslims fast and seek Allah.

16 **https://www.unrefugees.org/refugee-facts/what-is-a-refugee/**

17 **https://www.rnz.co.nz/news/chch-terror/385863/christchurch-mosque-attack-survivor-farid-ahmed-i-have-chosen-love-and-i-have-forgiven**

About the Author

Nick Regnault is the Resettlement Coordinator for South West Baptist Church. His church was one of four approved community sponsors in the pilot Community Organisation Refugee Sponsorship programme. He co-ordinates the many volunteers that have contributed to welcoming former refugee families into Christchurch.

Since mid-2017 he has been working with local and global organisations and passionate individuals to engage with the government and establish a permanent programme for communities to welcome refugees into Aotearoa New Zealand.